22   ems

E. E. CUMMINGS

Edited by George James Firmage

Liveright

New York • London

First published as a Liveright paperback 2001

Printed in the United States of America

Library of Congress Cataloging-in-Publication Data

Cummings, E. E. (Edward Estlin), 1894–1962.
    22 and 50 poems / E.E. Cummings ; edited by George James Firmage.
    p. cm.
    Includes bibliographical references.
    ISBN 0-87140-177-0 (pbk.)
    I. Title: Twenty-two and fifty poems. II. Firmage, George James. III.
Title.
PS3505.U334 A6 2001
811'.52—dc21

                                                              00-039118

Liveright Publishing Corporation
500 Fifth Avenue, New York, N.Y. 10110

W. W. Norton & Company Ltd.
10 Coptic Street, London WC1A 1PU

1   2   3   4   5   6   7   8   9   0

CONTENTS

New Poems [from Collected Poems] (1938)

50 Poems (1940)

7

New Poems

[from COLLECTED POEMS]

INTRODUCTION

The poems to come are for you and for me and are not for mostpeople
—it's no use trying to pretend that mostpeople and ourselves are
alike. Mostpeople have less in common with ourselves than the
squarerootofminusone. You and I are human beings;mostpeople are
snobs. Take the matter of being born. What does being born mean to
mostpeople? Catastrophe unmitigated. Socialrevolution. The
cultured aristocrat yanked out of his hyperexclusively ultravolup-
tuous superpalazzo,and dumped into an incredibly vulgar deten-
tioncamp swarming with every conceivable species of undesirable
organism. Mostpeople fancy a guaranteed birthproof safetysuit
of nondestructible selflessness. If mostpeople were to be born twice
they'd improbably call it dying—
you and I are not snobs. We can never be born enough. We are
human beings;for whom birth is a supremely welcome mystery,the
mystery of growing:the mystery which happens only and whenever
we are faithful to ourselves. You and I wear the dangerous looseness
of doom and find it becoming. Life,for eternal us,is now;and now
is much too busy being a little more than everything to seem any-
thing,catastrophic included.

Life,for mostpeople,simply isn't. Take the socalled standard-
ofliving. What do mostpeople mean by "living"? They don't mean
living. They mean the latest and closest plural approximation to
singular prenatal passivity which science,in its finite but unbounded
wisdom,has succeeded in selling their wives. If science could fail,a
mountain's a mammal. Mostpeople's wives can spot a genuine delu-

sion of embryonic omnipotence immediately and will accept no substitutes

—luckily for us,a mountain is a mammal. The plusorminus movie to end moving,the strictly scientific parlourgame of real unreality,the tyranny conceived in misconception and dedicated to the proposition that every man is a woman and any woman a king,hasn't a wheel to stand on. What their most synthetic not to mention transparent majesty, mrsandmr collective foetus,would improbably call a ghost is walking. He isn't an undream of anaesthetized impersons,or a cosmic comfortstation,or a transcendentally sterilized lookiesoundiefeelietastiesmellie. He is a healthily complex,a naturally homogeneous,citizen of immortality. The now of his each pitying free imperfect gesture,his any birth or breathing,insults perfected inframortally millenniums of slavishness. He is a little more than everything,he is democracy;he is alive:he is ourselves.

Miracles are to come. With you I leave a remembrance of miracles:they are by somebody who can love and who shall be continually reborn, a human being;somebody who said to those near him,when his fingers would not hold a brush "tie it into my hand"—

nothing proving or sick or partial. Nothing false,nothing difficult or easy or small or colossal. Nothing ordinary or extraordinary, nothing emptied or filled,real or unreal;nothing feeble and known or clumsy and guessed. Everywhere tints childrening,innocent spontaneous,true. Nowhere possibly what flesh and impossibly such a garden,but actually flowers which breasts are among the very mouths of light. Nothing believed or doubted;brain over heart, surface:nowhere hating or to fear; shadow,mind without soul. Only how measureless cool flames of making; only each other building always distinct selves of mutual entirely opening;only alive. Never the murdered finalities of wherewhen and yesno, impotent nongames of wrongright and rightwrong;never to gain or pause,never the soft adventure of undoom,greedy anguishes and cringing ecstasies of inexistence;never to rest and never to have:only to grow.

Always the beautiful answer who asks a more beautiful question

E. E. CUMMINGS

|

un
der fog
's
touch

slo

ings
fin
gering
s

wli

whichs
turn
in
to whos

est

people
be
come
un

2

kind)
YM&WC
(of sort of)
A soursweet bedtime

-less un-
(wonderful)
story atrickling a
-rithmetic o-

ver me you & all those & that
"I may say professor"
asleep
wop "shapley

has compared the universe
to a
uh" pause
"Cookie

but" nonvisibly smi-
ling through man
-ufactured harmlessly accurate
gloom "I

think he might now be inclined to describe
it rather as
a" pause "uh"
cough

"Biscuit"
(& so on & so unto canned
swoonsong
came "I wish you good" the mechanical

dawn
"morning")& that those you
i St
ep

into the not
merely immeasurable into
the mightily alive the
dear beautiful eternal night

3

a football with white eyebrows the
3
rd chief something or must be off

duty wanderfuling aft spits)
int
o immensity(upon once whom

fiercely by pink mr seized green
mrs
opening is it horribly smith spouts

cornucopiously not unrecognizable whats of
t
oo vertiginously absorbed which à la

4

(of Ever-Ever Land i speak
sweet morons gather roun'
who does not dare to stand or sit
may take it lying down)

down with the human soul
and anything else uncanned
for everyone carries canopeners
in Ever-Ever Land

(for Ever-Ever Land is a place
that's as simple as simple can be
and was built that way on purpose
by simple people like we)

down with hell and heaven
and all the religious fuss
infinity pleased our parents
one inch looks good to us

(and Ever-Ever Land is a place
that's measured and safe and known
where it's lucky to be unlucky
and the hitler lies down with the cohn)

down above all with love
and everything perverse
or which makes some feel more better
when all ought to feel less worse

(but only sameness is normal
in Ever-Ever Land
for a bad cigar is a woman
but a gland is only a gland)

5

lucky means finding
Holes where
pockets aren't lucky
's to spend

laughter
not money lucky are
Breathe
grow dream

die love not
Fear eat sleep kill
and have you am luck
-y is we lucky luck-

ier
luck
-I-
est

6

Q:dwo
  we know of anything which can
  be as dull as one englishman
A:to

7

&-moon-He-be-hind-a-mills

tosses like thin bums dream
ing i'm thick in a hot young queen with

a twot with a twitch like kingdom
come(moon
The

sq
uirmwri
th-ing out of wonderful
thunder!of?ocean.a

ndn
ooneandfor
e-ver)moon She over this new eng
land fragrance of pasture and now ti

p toe ingt o
a child who alone st
and

s(not a
fraid of moon You)

not-mere-ly-won-der-ing-&

8

this little bride & groom are
standing)in a kind
of crown he dressed
in black candy she

veiled with candy white
carrying a bouquet of
pretend flowers this
candy crown with this candy

little bride & little
groom in it kind of stands on
a thin ring which stands on a much
less thin very much more

big & kinder of ring & which
kinder of stands on a
much more than very much
biggest & thickest & kindest

of ring & all one two three rings
are cake & everything is protected by
cellophane against anything(because
nothing really exists

9

so little he is
so.
     Little
ness be

(ing)
comes ex
-pert-
Ly expand:grO

w
 i
?n
  g

Is poet iS
(childlost
so;ul
)foundclown a

-live a
,bird
    !O
& j &

ji
&
jim,jimm
;jimmy

s:
  A
V
o(

   .
    :
     ;
     ,

nor woman
     (just as it be

       gan to snow he dis
        a

        ppeare
        d leavi
         ng on its

          elf pro
           pped uprigh
           t that in this o
          ther w

         ise how e
        mpty park bundl
        e of what man can

      't hurt any more h
     u
      sh
nor child)

11

my specialty is living said
a man(who could not earn his bread
because he would not sell his head)

squads right impatiently replied
two billion pubic lice inside
one pair of trousers(which had died)

12

The Mind's(

i never you never
he she or it

never we you and they never
saw so
much heard so much smelled so much

tasted
plus touched quite so And
How much nonexistence
eye sed bea

yew tea mis
eyesucks unyewkuntel finglestein idstings
yewrety oride lesgo eckshun

kemeruh daretoi
nig

)Ah,Soul

if i

or anybody don't
know where it her his

my next meal's coming from
i say to hell with that
that doesn't matter(and if

he she it or everybody gets a
bellyful without
lifting my finger i say to hell
with that i

say that doesn't matter)but
if somebody
or you are beautiful or
deep or generous what
i say is

whistle that
sing that yell that spell
that out big(bigger than cosmic
rays war earthquakes famine or the ex

prince of whoses diving into
a whatses to rescue miss nobody's
probably handbag)because i say that's not

swell(get me)babe not(understand me)lousy
kid that's something else my sweet(i feel that's

true)

14

hanged

if n
y in a real hot spell
with o

man

what bubbies going
places on such
babies aint plenty
good enough for

i

eu
can have
you

rope

15

economic secu
rity" is a cu
rious excu

se
(in

use among pu
rposive pu
nks)for pu

tting the arse
before the torse

16

beware beware beware
because because because
equals(transparent or

science must
bait laws with
stars to catch telescopes

)why.
Being is
patience is patient is(patiently

all the eyes of these with listening
hands only fishermen are
prevented by cathedrals

only as what(out of a flophouse)floats
on murdered feet into immense no

Where
            which to map while these not eyes quite try
almost their mind immeasurably roots
among much soundless rubbish of guitars
and watches
            only as this(which might have been
a man and kept a date and played a tune)
death's dollhead wandering under weakening stars

Feels;if
            & god said & there was
                                    is born:
one face who.
            and hands hold his whose unlife
bursts

        only so;only if you should turn
the infinite corner of love,all that i am
easily disappears(leaving no proof

not the least shadow of a.   Not one smallest dream)

must being shall

one only thing must:the opening of a
(not some not every but any)
heart—wholly,idiotically—before
such nonsense which
is the overlove & underwish of
beauty;before keen if
dim quiveringly
spangle & thingless
& before flashing soft neverwheres &
sweet nothingly gushing tinsel;silently
yes before angel curvings upon a mostless
more of star

o-

pening of(writhing your exploding my)heart
before how worlds delicate
of bombast—papery what
& vast solidities,unwinding
dizzily &
mirrors;sprung dimensionless
new alls of joy:quietly & before illimitably
spiralling candy of tiniest
forever—crazily from totally sprouted by alive
green each very lifting
& seriously voice
-like finger of

the tree

may my heart always be open to little
birds who are the secrets of living
whatever they sing is better than to know
and if men should not hear them men are old

may my mind stroll about hungry
and fearless and thirsty and supple
and even if it's sunday may i be wrong
for whenever men are right they are not young

and may myself do nothing usefully
and love yourself so more than truly
there's never been quite such a fool who could fail
pulling all the sky over him with one smile

20

the people who
rain(are move as)proces
-sion Its of like immens-
ely(a feet which is prayer

among)float withins he
upclimbest And(sky she
)open new(
dark we all findingly Spring the

Fragrance unvisible)ges
-tured together-
ly singing ams
trample(they flyingly silence

21

porky & porkie
sit into a moon)

blacker than dreams
are round like a spoon are
both making silence

two–made–of–one

& nothing tells anywhere
"snow will come soon" &
pretending they're birds sit

creatures of quills
(asleep who must go

things-without-wings

22

you shall above all things be glad and young.
For if you're young,whatever life you wear

it will become you;and if you are glad
whatever's living will yourself become.
Girlboys may nothing more than boygirls need:
i can entirely her only love

whose any mystery makes every man's
flesh put space on;and his mind take off time

that you should ever think,may god forbid
and(in his mercy)your true lover spare:
for that way knowledge lies,the foetal grave
called progress,and negation's dead undoom.

I'd rather learn from one bird how to sing
than teach ten thousand stars how not to dance

50 POEMS

to m. m.

l

!blac
k
agains
t

(whi)

te sky
?t
rees whic
h fr

om droppe

d

,
le
af

a:;go

e
s wh
IrlI
n

.g

2

fl

a
tt
ene

d d

reaml
essn
esse

s wa

it
sp
i

t)(t

he
s
e

f

ooli
sh sh
apes

ccocoucougcoughcoughi

ng with me
n more o
n than in the

m

3

If you can't eat you got to

smoke and we aint got
nothing to smoke:come on kid

let's go to sleep
if you can't smoke you got to

Sing and we aint got

nothing to sing;come on kid
let's go to sleep

if you can't sing you got to
die and we aint got

Nothing to die,come on kid

let's go to sleep
if you can't die you got to

dream and we aint got
nothing to dream(come on kid

Let's go to sleep)

4

nobody loved this
he)with its
of eye stuck
into a rock of

forehead.No
body

loved
big that quick
sharp
thick snake of a

voice these

root
like legs
or
feethands;

nobody
ever could ever

had love loved whose his
climbing shoulders queerly twilight
:never,no
(body.

Nothing

5

am was.   are leaves few this.   is these a or
scratchily over which of earth dragged once
-ful leaf.   & were who skies clutch an of poor
how colding hereless.   air theres what immense
live without every dancing.   singless on-
ly a child's eyes float silently down
more than two those that and that noing our
gone snow gone
                    yours mine
                        . We're
alive and shall be:cities may overflow(am
was)assassinating whole grassblades,five
ideas can swallow a man;three words im
-prison a woman for all her now:but we've
such freedom such intense digestion so
much greenness only dying makes us grow

flotsam and jetsam
are gentlemen poeds
urseappeal netsam
our spinsters and coeds)

thoroughly bretish
they scout the inhuman
itarian fetish
that man isn't wuman

vive the millenni
um three cheers for labor
give all things to enni
one bugger thy nabor

(neck and senecktie
are gentlemen ppoyds
even whose recktie
are covered by lloyd's

moan
(is)
ing

the she of the
sea
un

der a who
a he a moon a
magic out

of the black this which of
one street leaps quick
squirmthicklying lu

minous night
mare som
e w

hereanynoevery
ing(danc)ing
wills&weres

8

the Noster was a ship of swank
(as gallant as they come)
until she hit a mine and sank
just off the coast of Sum

precisely where a craft of cost
the Ergo perished later
all hands(you may recall)being lost
including captain Pater

9

warped this perhapsy
stumbl
i
NgflounderpirouettiN
                    g

:seized(

tatterdemalion
dow
      nupfloatsw
                oon
InG

s ly)tuck.s its(ghostsoul sheshape)

elf into leasting forever most
magical maybes of certainly
never the iswas

teetertiptotterish

sp-
   inwhirlpin
              -wh
EEling
;a!who,

(

whic hbubble ssomethin
gabou tlov
e)

10

spoke joe to jack

leave her alone
she's not your gal

jack spoke to joe
's left crashed
pal dropped

o god alice
yells but who shot
up grabbing had
by my throat me

give it him good
a bottle she
quick who stop damned
fall all we go spill

and chairs tables the and
bitch whispers jill
mopping too bad

dear sh not yet
jesus what blood

darling i said

| |

red-rag and pink-flag
blackshirt and brown
strut-mince and stink-brag
have all come to town

some like it shot
and some like it hung
and some like it in the twot
nine months young

12

(will you teach a
wretch to live
straighter than a needle)

ask
    her
        ask
            when
                (ask and
                ask
                and ask
again and)ask a
brittle little
person fiddling
in
the
rain

(did you kiss
a girl with nipples
like pink thimbles)

ask
    him
        ask
            who
                (ask and
                ask
                and ask
ago and)ask a
simple
crazy
thing
singing
in the snow

13

proud of his scientific attitude

and liked the prince of wales wife wants to die
but the doctors won't let her comma considers frood
whom he pronounces young mistaken and
cradles in rubbery one somewhat hand
the paper destinies of nations sic
item a bounceless period unshy
the empty house is full O Yes of guk
rooms daughter item son a woopsing queer
colon hobby photography never has plumbed
the heights of prowst but respects artists if
they are sincere proud of his scientif
ic attitude and liked the king of)hear

ye!the godless are the dull and the dull are the damned

the way to hump a cow is not
to get yourself a stool
but draw a line around the spot
and call it beautifool

to multiply because and why
dividing thens by nows
and adding and(i understand)
is hows to hump a cows

the way to hump a cow is not
to elevate your tool
but drop a penny in the slot
and bellow like a bool

to lay a wreath from ancient greath
on insulated brows
(while tossing boms at uncle toms)
is hows to hump a cows

the way to hump a cow is not
to push and then to pull
but practicing the art of swot
to preach the golden rull

to vote for me(all decent mem
and wonens will allows
which if they don't to hell with them)
is hows to hump a cows

mrs

& mr across the way are kind of
afraid)afraid

of what(of

a crazy man)don't
ask me how i know(a he of head
comes to some dirty window every)twilight i

feel(his lousy eyes roaming)wonderful all

sky(a little mouth)stumbling(can't
keep up with how big very
them)now(it tears
off rag its

of

mind chucks away flimsy
which but)always(they're
more much further off)further these
those three disappear finally what's left

behind is(just a head of he

is)merely(a pair of ears with some
lips plus a couple of)holes probably that's what
(mr & mrs are

sort of really

really kind
of afraid of)these(down pull & who'll

shades

)when what hugs stopping earth than silent is
more silent than more than much more is or
total sun oceaning than any this
tear jumping from each most least eye of star

and without was if minus and shall be
immeasurable happenless unnow
shuts more than open could that every tree
or than all life more death begins to grow

end's ending then these dolls of joy and grief
these recent memories of future dream
these perhaps who have lost their shadows if
which did not do the losing spectres mime

until out of merely not nothing comes
only one snowflake(and we speak our names

youful

larger
of smallish)

Humble a
rosily
,nimblest;

c-urlin-g
noworld
Silent is

blue
(sleep!new

girlgold

18

ecco a letter starting "dearest we"
unsigned:remarkably brief but covering
one complete miracle of nearest far

"i cordially invite me to become
noone except yourselves r s v p"

she cannot read or write,la moon.   Employs
a very crazily how clownlike that
this quickly ghost scribbling from there to where

—name unless i'm mistaken chauvesouris—
whose grammar is atrocious;but so what

princess selene doesn't know a thing
who's much too busy being her beautiful yes.
The place is now
                        let us accept
                                  (the time

forever,and you'll wear your silver shoes

19

there is a here and

that here was a
town(and the town is

so aged the ocean
wanders the streets are so
ancient the houses enter the

people are so feeble the feeble go to
sleep if the people sit down)
and this light is so dark the mountains
grow up from

the sky is so near the earth does not
open her
eyes(but the
feeble are people the feeble
are so wise the people

remember being born)
when and
if nothing disappears they
will disappear always who are filled

with never are more than
more is are mostly
almost are feebler than feeble are

fable who are less than these are least is who
are am(beyond when behind where under

un)

20

harder perhaps than a newengland bed

these ends of arms which pinch that purple book
between what hands had been before they died

squirming:now withered and unself her gnarled
vomits a rock of mindscream into life;
possibly darker than a spinster's heart

my voice feels who inquires is your cough
better today?nn-nn went head face goes

(if how begins a pillow's green means face

or why a quilt's pink stops might equal head).
Then with the splendor of an angel's fart

came one trembling out of huge each eye look
"thank you" nicely the lady's small grin said
(with more simplicity than makes a world)

21

six

are in a room's dark around)
five

(are all dancesing singdance all are

three
with faces made of cloud dancing and
three
singing with voices made of earth and

six are in a room's dark around)

five
(six are in a room's)
one

is red

and(six are in)
four are

white

(three singdance six dancesing three
all around around all
clouds singing three and
and three dancing earths

three menandwomen three

and all around all and
all around five all
around five around)

five flowers five

(six are in a room's dark)
all five are one

flowers five flowers and all one is fire

22

nouns to nouns

wan
wan

too nons too

and
and

nuns two nuns

w an d
ering

in sin

g
ular untheknowndulous s

pring

23

a pretty a day
(and every fades)
is here and away
(but born are maids
to flower an hour
in all,all)

o yes to flower
until so blithe
a doer a wooer
some limber and lithe
some very fine mower
a tall;tall

some jerry so very
(and nellie and fan)
some handsomest harry
(and sally and nan
they tremble and cower
so pale:pale)

for betty was born
to never say nay
but lucy could learn
and lily could pray
and fewer were shyer
than doll.   doll

24

these people socalled were not given hearts
how should they be?their socalled hearts would think
these socalled people have no minds but if
they had their minds socalled would not exist

but if these not existing minds took life
such life could not begin to live id est
breathe but if such life could its breath would stink

and as for souls why souls are wholes not parts
but all these hundreds upon thousands of
people socalled if multiplied by twice
infinity could never equal one)

which may your million selves and my suffice
to through the only mystery of love
become while every sun goes round its moon

as freedom is a breakfastfood
or truth can live with right and wrong
or molehills are from mountains made
—long enough and just so long
will being pay the rent of seem
and genius please the talentgang
and water most encourage flame

as hatracks into peachtrees grow
or hopes dance best on bald men's hair
and every finger is a toe
and any courage is a fear
—long enough and just so long
will the impure think all things pure
and hornets wail by children stung

or as the seeing are the blind
and robins never welcome spring
nor flatfolk prove their world is round
nor dingsters die at break of dong
and common's rare and millstones float
—long enough and just so long
tomorrow will not be too late

worms are the words but joy's the voice
down shall go which and up come who
breasts will be breasts thighs will be thighs
deeds cannot dream what dreams can do
—time is a tree(this life one leaf)
but love is the sky and i am for you
just so long and long enough

26

wherelings whenlings
(daughters of ifbut offspring of hopefear
sons of unless and children of almost)
never shall guess the dimension of

him whose
each
foot likes the
here of this earth

whose both
eyes
love
this now of the sky

—endlings of isn't
shall never
begin
to begin to

imagine how(only are shall be were
dawn dark rain snow rain
-bow &
a

moon
's whis-
per
in sunset

or thrushes toward dusk among whippoorwills or
tree field rock hollyhock forest brook chickadee
mountain.   Mountain)
whycoloured worlds of because do

not stand against yes which is built by
forever & sunsmell
(sometimes a wonder
of wild roses

sometimes)
with north
over
the barn

buy me an ounce and i'll sell you a pound.
Turn
gert
    (spin!
helen)the
slimmer the finger the thicker the thumb(it's
whirl,
girls)
round and round

early to better is wiser for worse.
Give
liz
    (take!
tommy)we
order a steak and they send us a pie(it's
try,
boys)
mine is yours

ask me the name of the moon in the man.
Up
sam
    (down!
alice)a
hole in the ocean will never be missed(it's
in,
girls)
yours is mine

either was deafer than neither was dumb.
Skip
fred
    (jump!
neddy)but

under the wonder is over the why(it's
now,
boys)
here we come

28

there are possibly 2½ or impossibly 3
individuals every several fat
thousand years.   Expecting more would be
neither fantastic nor pathological but

dumb.   The number of times a wheel turns
doesn't determine its roundness:if swallows tryst
in your barn be glad;nobody ever earns
anything, everything little looks big in a mist

and if(by Him Whose blood was for us spilled)
than all mankind something more small occurs
or something more distorting than socalled
civilization i'll kiss a stalinist arse

in hitler's window on wednesday next at 1
E.S.T. bring the kiddies let's all have fun

29

anyone lived in a pretty how town
(with up so floating many bells down)
spring summer autumn winter
he sang his didn't he danced his did.

Women and men(both little and small)
cared for anyone not at all
they sowed their isn't they reaped their same
sun moon stars rain

children guessed(but only a few
and down they forgot as up they grew
autumn winter spring summer)
that noone loved him more by more

when by now and tree by leaf
she laughed his joy she cried his grief
bird by snow and stir by still
anyone's any was all to her

someones married their everyones
laughed their cryings and did their dance
(sleep wake hope and then)they
said their nevers they slept their dream

stars rain sun moon
(and only the snow can begin to explain
how children are apt to forget to remember
with up so floating many bells down)

one day anyone died i guess
(and noone stooped to kiss his face)
busy folk buried them side by side
little by little and was by was

all by all and deep by deep
and more by more they dream their sleep
noone and anyone earth by april
wish by spirit and if by yes.

Women and men(both dong and ding)
summer autumn winter spring
reaped their sowing and went their came
sun moon stars rain

the silently little blue elephant shyly(he was terri
bly
warped by his voyage from every to no)who
still stands still as found some lost thing(like a
curtain on which tiny the was painted in round
blue but quite now it's swirly and foldish so only through)the
little blue elephant at the zoo(jumbled
to queer this what that a here and
there a peers at you)has(elephant the blue)put some just
a now and now little the(on his quiet
head his magical shoulders him doll
self)hay completely thus or that wispily
is to say according to his perfect
satisfaction vanishing from a this world into bigger
much some out of(not visible to us)whom only his dream
ing own soul looks
and
the is all floatful and remembering

31

not time's how(anchored in what mountaining roots
of mere eternity)stupendous if
discoverably disappearing floats
at trillionworlded the ecstatic ease

with which vast my complexly wisdoming friend's
—a fingery treesoul onlying from serene
whom queries not suspected selves of space—
life stands gradually upon four minds

(out of some undering joy and overing grief
nothing arrives a so prodigious am
a so immediate is escorts us home
through never's always until absolute un

gulps the first knowledge of death's wandering guess)
while children climb their eyes to touch his dream

32

newlys of silence
(both an only

moon the with star

one moving are twilight
they beyond near)

girlest she slender

is cradling in joy her
flower than now

(softlying wisdoms

enter guess)
childmoon smile to

your breathing doll

33

one slipslouch twi
tterstamp
coon wid a plon
kykerplung
guit
ar
  (pleez make me glad)dis

dumdam slamslum slopp
idy wurl
sho am
wick
id id
ar
  (now heer we kum dearie)bud

hooz
gwine ter
hate
dad hurt
fool wurl no gal no
boy
    (day simbully loves id)fer

ids dare
pain dares un
no
budy elses un ids
dare dare
joy
  (eye kinely thank yoo)

34

my father moved through dooms of love
through sames of am through haves of give,
singing each morning out of each night
my father moved through depths of height

this motionless forgetful where
turned at his glance to shining here;
that if(so timid air is firm)
under his eyes would stir and squirm

newly as from unburied which
floats the first who,his april touch
drove sleeping selves to swarm their fates
woke dreamers to their ghostly roots

and should some why completely weep
my father's fingers brought her sleep:
vainly no smallest voice might cry
for he could feel the mountains grow.

Lifting the valleys of the sea
my father moved through griefs of joy;
praising a forehead called the moon
singing desire into begin

joy was his song and joy so pure
a heart of star by him could steer
and pure so now and now so yes
the wrists of twilight would rejoice

keen as midsummer's keen beyond
conceiving mind of sun will stand,
so strictly(over utmost him
so hugely)stood my father's dream

his flesh was flesh his blood was blood:
no hungry man but wished him food;
no cripple wouldn't creep one mile
uphill to only see him smile.

Scorning the pomp of must and shall
my father moved through dooms of feel;
his anger was as right as rain
his pity was as green as grain

septembering arms of year extend
less humbly wealth to foe and friend
than he to foolish and to wise
offered immeasurable is

proudly and(by octobering flame
beckoned)as earth will downward climb,
so naked for immortal work
his shoulders marched against the dark

his sorrow was as true as bread:
no liar looked him in the head;
if every friend became his foe
he'd laugh and build a world with snow.

My father moved through theys of we,
singing each new leaf out of each tree
(and every child was sure that spring
danced when she heard my father sing)

then let men kill which cannot share,
let blood and flesh be mud and mire,
scheming imagine,passion willed,
freedom a drug that's bought and sold

giving to steal and cruel kind,
a heart to fear,to doubt a mind,

to differ a disease of same,
conform the pinnacle of am

though dull were all we taste as bright,
bitter all utterly things sweet,
maggoty minus and dumb death
all we inherit,all bequeath

and nothing quite so least as truth
—i say though hate were why men breathe—
because my father lived his soul
love is the whole and more than all

35

you which could grin three smiles into a dead
house clutch between eyes emptiness toss one

at nobody shoulder and thick stickingly un

stride after glide massacre monday did
more)ask a lifelump buried by the star
nicked ends next among broken odds of yes
terday's tomorrow(than today can guess

or fears to dare whatever dares to fear)

i very humbly thank you which could grin
may stern particular Love surround your trite
how terrible self hood with its hands and feet

(lift and may pitying Who from sharp soft worms

of spiralling why and out of black because
your absolute courage with its legs and arms

i say no world

can hold a you
shall see the not
because
and why but
(who
stood within his steam be-
ginning and
began to sing all
here is hands machine no

good too quick i know this
suit you pay
a store too
much yes what
too much o much cheap
me i work i know i say i have
not any
never
no vacation here

is hands is work since i am
born is good
but there this cheap this suit too
quick no suit there every
-thing
nothing i
say the
world not fit
you)he is

not(i say the world
yes any world is much
too not quite big enough to

hold one tiny this with
time's
more than
most how
immeasurable
anguish

pregnant one fearless
one good yes
completely kind
mindheart one true one generous child-
man
-god one eager
souldoll one
unsellable not buyable alive
one i say human being)one

goldberger

37

these children singing in stone a
silence of stone these
little children wound with stone
flowers opening for

ever these silently lit
tle children are petals
their song is a flower of
always their flowers

of stone are
silently singing
a song more silent
than silence these always

children forever
singing wreathed with singing
blossoms children of
stone with blossoming

eyes
know if a
lit tle
tree listens

forever to always children singing forever
a song made
of silent as stone silence of
song

38

love is the every only god

who spoke this earth so glad and big
even a thing all small and sad
man,may his mighty briefness dig

for love beginning means return
seas who could sing so deep and strong

one querying wave will whitely yearn
from each last shore and home come young

so truly perfectly the skies
by merciful love whispered were,
completes its brightness with your eyes

any illimitable star

39

denied night's face
have shadowless they?
i bring you peace
the moon of day

predicted end
who never began
of god and fiend?
i give you man

extracted hate
from whispering grass?
joy in time shut
and starved on space?

love's murdered eye
dissected to mere
because and why?
take this whole tear.

By handless hints
do conjurers rule?
do mannikins
forbid the soul?

is death a whore
with life's disease
which quacks will cure
when pimps may please?

must through unstrange
synthetic now
true histories plunge?
rains a grey snow

of mothery same
rotting keen dream?
i rise which am
the sun of whom

40

a peopleshaped toomany-ness far too

and will it tell us who we are and will
it tell us why we dream and will it tell
us how we drink crawl eat walk die fly do?

a notalive undead too-nearishness

and shall we cry and shall we laugh and shall
entirely our doom steer his great small
wish into upward deepness of less fear
much than more climbing hope meets most despair?

all knowing's having and have is(you guess)
perhaps the very unkindest way to kill
each of those creatures called one's self so we'll

not have(but i imagine that yes is
the only living thing)and we'll make yes

up into the silence the green
silence with a white earth in it

you will(kiss me)go

out into the morning the young
morning with a warm world in it

(kiss me)you will go

on into the sunlight the fine
sunlight with a firm day in it

you will go(kiss me

down into your memory and
a memory and memory

i)kiss me(will go)

42

love is more thicker than forget
more thinner than recall
more seldom than a wave is wet
more frequent than to fail

it is most mad and moonly
and less it shall unbe
than all the sea which only
is deeper than the sea

love is less always than to win
less never than alive
less bigger than the least begin
less littler than forgive

it is most sane and sunly
and more it cannot die
than all the sky which only
is higher than the sky

43

hate blows a bubble of despair into
hugeness world system universe and bang
—fear buries a tomorrow under woe
and up comes yesterday most green and young

pleasure and pain are merely surfaces
(one itself showing,itself hiding one)
life's only and true value neither is
love makes the little thickness of the coin

comes here a man would have from madame death
neverless now and without winter spring?
she'll spin that spirit her own fingers with
and give him nothing(if he should not sing)

how much more than enough for both of us
darling.   And if i sing you are my voice,

44

air,

be
comes
or

(a)

new
(live)
now

;&

th
(is no littler
th

an a:

fear no bigger
th
an a

hope)is

st
anding
st

a.r

enters give
whose lost is his found
leading love
whose heart is her mind)

supremely whole
uplifting the,
of each where all
was is to be

welcomes welcomes
her dreams his face
(her face his dreams
rejoice rejoice)

—opens the sun:
who music wear
burst icy known
swim ignorant fire

(adventuring
and time's dead which;
falling falling
both locked in each

down a thief by
a whore dragged goes
to meet her why
she his because

46

grEEn's d

an
cing on hollow was

young Up
floatingly clothes tumbledish
olD(with

sprouts o
ver and)a-
live
wanders remembe

r
ing per
F
ectl
y

crumb
ling eye
-holes oUt of whe
reful whom(leas

tly)
smiles the
infinite nothing

of
M

an

47

(sitting in a tree-)
o small you
sitting in a tree-

sitting in a treetop

riding on a greenest

riding on a greener
(o little i)
riding on a leaf

o least who
sing small thing
dance little joy

(shine most prayer)

48

mortals)

climbi
      ng i
      nto eachness begi
      n
dizzily
        swingthings
of speeds of
trapeze gush somersaults
open ing
        hes shes
&meet&
      swoop
          fully is are ex
                  quisite theys of re
turn
   a
   n
   d
fall which now drop who all dreamlike

(im

49

i am so glad and very
merely my fourth will cure
the laziest self of weary
the hugest sea of shore

so far your nearness reaches
a lucky fifth of you
turns people into eachs
and cowards into grow

our can'ts were born to happen
our mosts have died in more
our twentieth will open
wide a wide open door

we are so both and oneful
night cannot be so sky
sky cannot be so sunful
i am through you so i

50

what freedom's not some under's mere above
but breathing yes which fear will never no?
measureless our pure living complete love
whose doom is beauty and its fate to grow

shall hate confound the wise?doubt blind the brave?
does mask wear face?have singings gone to say?
here youngest selves yet younger selves conceive
here's music's music and the day of day

are worlds collapsing?any was a glove
but i'm and you are actual either hand
is when for sale?forever is to give
and on forever's very now we stand

nor a first rose explodes but shall increase
whole truthful infinite immediate us

AFTERWORD

The twenty-two "New Poems" from *"Collected*(wrongly:rightly *Selected)Poems"*,[1] as Cummings referred to the volume published in 1938, and *50 Poems*, which appeared two years later, were both issued through the good offices of Charles A. Pearce, an editor at Harcourt, Brace and Company during the 1930s who subsequently joined the firm of Duell, Sloan and Pearce in 1939.

According to Pearce, it was sometime in the spring of 1937 that he "proposed a COMPLETE book (of all the published poems), but e. e. c. made the decision to limit it. . . ." The idea for the book "met with somewhat reluctant approval" at Harcourt, "but turned out well in the long run."[2]

When Pearce joined Duell, Sloan and Pearce a year after the publication of *Collected Poems*, he asked Cummings to help him celebrate his new association with a new volume of poetry. The poet obliged with the manuscript of *50 Poems* early in 1940. In December that year, a signed edition limited to 150 copies was issued. A regular trade edition followed in January 1941. "m.m." is Marion Morehouse, Cummings's third wife.

The texts and settings of the "Introduction" to *Collected Poems*, the "New Poems" and *50 Poems* are based on the poet's typescripts in the Houghton Library, Harvard University.

GEORGE JAMES FIRMAGE

1. *Selected Letters of E. E. Cummings*, edited by F. W. Dupee and George Stade (New York, 1969), p. 165.
2. *The Magic-Maker: E. E. Cummings*, by Charles Norman (New York, 1958), p. 310.